NBA CHAMPIONSHIP:

1978

ALL-TIME LEADING SCORER:

ELVIN HAYES (1972–81):

15,551 POINTS

THE NBA: A HISTORY OF HOOPS

WASHINGTON WIZARDS

Abe
WIZARDS
7

THE NBA: A HISTORY OF HOOPS

WASHINGTON WIZARDS

BY JIM WHITING

CREATIVE EDUCATION CREATIVE PAPERBACKS

Published by Creative Education
and Creative Paperbacks
P.O. Box 227, Mankato, Minnesota 56002
Creative Education and Creative Paperbacks
are imprints of The Creative Company
www.thecreativecompany.us

Design by Blue Design;
production by Chelsey Luther
Printed in the United States of America

Photographs by Alamy (David Blair/ZUMA Wire/Alamy Live News/ZUMA Press, Inc., B Christopher, Christopher Szagola/Cal Sport Media), Corbis (Bettmann, Charles Tasnadi/AP), Dreamstime (Chrishowey), Getty Images (Bill Baptist/NBAE, Vernon Biever/NBAE, Nathaniel S. Butler/NBAE, Ned Dishman/NBAE, Stephen M. Dowell/Orlando Sentinel/MCT/Tribune News Service, G Fiume/Getty Images Sport, Focus on Sport, George Gojkovich/Getty Images Sport, Walter Iooss Jr./Sports Illustrated, Doug Pensinger/Getty Images Sport, Dick Raphael/NBAE, Vincent Riehl/New York Daily News Archive, Toni L. Sandys/The Washington Post, Tony Triolo/Sports Illustrated, Jerry Wachter/NBAE)

Library of Congress Cataloging-in-Publication Data
Names: Whiting, Jim, 1943- author.
Title: Washington Wizards / Jim Whiting.
Series: The NBA: A History of Hoops.
Includes bibliographical references and index.
Summary: This high-interest title summarizes the history of the Washington Wizards professional basketball team, highlighting memorable events and noteworthy players such as Westley Unseld.
Identifiers: LCCN 2017009416 / ISBN 978-1-60818-864-2 (hardcover) / ISBN 978-1-62832-467-9 (pbk) / ISBN 978-1-56660-912-8 (eBook)
Subjects: LCSH: 1. Washington Wizards (Basketball team)—History—Juvenile literature. 2. Washington Wizards (Basketball team)—Biography—Juvenile literature.
Classification: LCC GV885.52.W37 W55 2017 / DDC 796.323/6409753—dc23

CCSS: RI.4.1, 2, 3, 4; RI.5.1, 2, 4; RI.6.1, 2, 3; RF.4.3, 4; RF.5.3, 4; RH. 6-8. 4, 5, 7

First Edition HC 9 8 7 6 5 4 3 2 1
First Edition PBK 9 8 7 6 5 4 3 2 1

42
ROCKETS

Radio
Panasonic
bullets
24
43
38

CONTENTS

Since the 1800s, the nation's important issues have been discussed inside the U.S. Capitol in **WASHINGTON, D.C.**

CASTING THE BULLETS

To almost everyone in the Verizon Center in Washington, D.C., on December 8, 2014, the showdown between the Boston Celtics and Washington Wizards was simply another game in the long National

Basketball Association (NBA) season. To Wizards point guard John Wall, though, it was an evening of mourning. Nearly a year earlier, he had befriended Miyah Telemaque-Nelson. She was a six-year-old girl fighting cancer. Wall spent countless hours with Miyah. He arranged for her to meet her idol, singer Nicki Minaj. He wrote her name on his shoes. On this night, he had to change the message to RIP Miyah. She had died that morning. Wall played through his sorrow. He had a career-high 17 assists. The game went into double overtime. Then Wall took over. He scored his team's final 10 points. Washington won the game, 133–132. Wall broke down and cried at the post-game press conference. "This game was really meant for her," he said. "It would've been an even tougher day to lose it. I just went into a mode where I didn't want to lose this game."

Losing games began early for the Wizards. They began play in 1961. At that time, they were located in Chicago. Known as the

The top pick in the 2010 NBA Draft, **JOHN WALL** has proven his value in Washington.

LEGENDS OF THE HARDWOOD

HONEYCOMB

GUS JOHNSON, FORWARD, 6-FOOT-6, 1963–72

Gus Johnson's college coach Joe Cipriano nicknamed him "Honeycomb" because his game was so sweet. Not everyone shared that opinion. "Gus was probably one of the roughest players I have ever played against," said former New York Knicks star Dave DeBusschere. "But he was not a dirty player." During his career, Johnson was a five-time All-Star. But he played in an era before widespread media exposure. There is almost no film of his feats. He was virtually forgotten. Former players kept insisting he belonged in the Naismith Memorial Basketball Hall of Fame. Their persistence finally paid off. He was enshrined in 2010.

Packers, they were the NBA's first expansion franchise. The team was named for the city's meat-packing industry. The team didn't pack away many wins. The Packers' 18–62 record was the league's worst. Before the next season, they changed their name to Zephyrs. Zephyrus was the Greek god of the west wind. That was also an appropriate name. Chicago is nicknamed the "Windy City" for the strong breezes blowing off Lake Michigan. The Zephyrs barely improved, finishing with only 25 wins. That poor record didn't draw many fans. Team officials hoped a change of scenery would help improve things. They moved to Baltimore, Maryland, the following season.

The city was no stranger to pro hoops. A team called the Baltimore Bullets had joined the American Basketball League (ABL) in 1944. It was named "Bullets" because an ammunition factory was located

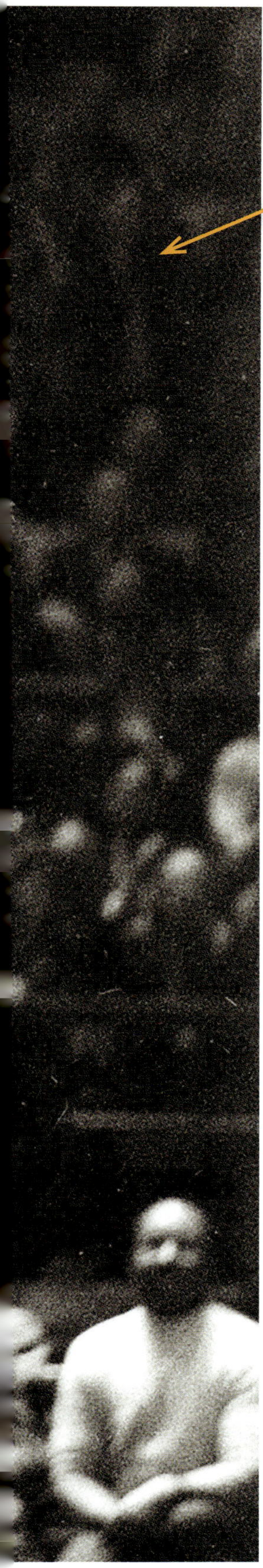

Forward **GUS JOHNSON** sometimes ripped the rim off the backboard with his powerful slam dunks.

nearby. Three years later, the Bullets joined the Basketball Association of America (BAA). They won the league title in their first season. Two years after that, the BAA merged with the National Basketball League (NBL). Together, they formed the NBA. The team consistently posted losing records in the NBA. It folded early in the 1954–55 season.

When the Zephyrs arrived in Baltimore, they took on the Bullets name. The new Bullets fired a lot of blanks the first season. They won only 31 games and didn't make the playoffs. But rugged forward Gus Johnson was runner-up for Rookie of the Year. His future teammate Earl Monroe said, "Gus was ahead of his time, flying through the air for slam dunks, breaking backboards, and throwing full-court passes behind his back. He was spectacular, but he also did the nitty-gritty jobs, defense and rebounding."

BECOMING WINNERS

Baltimore had a losing record again the following season. Yet it made the playoffs and nearly upset the heavily favored Los Angeles Lakers in the Western Division finals. Two years later, the Bullets won just 20 games. That gave them a high draft pick. They used it to take Monroe, a sensational point guard nicknamed "The Pearl." He was a real jewel.

Center **LEROY ELLIS** helped the Bullets reach the 1969 playoffs, but they could not beat the Knicks.

All-Star center **WES UNSELD** averaged 14 rebounds per game over 13 years with the Bullets.

He averaged more than 24 points a game. He was named Rookie of the Year. The following season, the Bullets drafted center Westley Unseld. He was Rookie of the Year *and* Most Valuable Player (MVP). Though he stood just 6-foot-7, he was immovable on defense and a dominant rebounder. “When we got Wes, we really got much better,” Monroe said. “It seemed like we got all the important rebounds. I think that gave us the impetus to know that we could win in this league.” And win they did.

LEGENDS OF THE HARDWOOD

AN EXCLUSIVE CLUB

WESTLEY UNSELD, CENTER, 6-FOOT-7, 1968–81

Westley Unseld was named Rookie of the Year and MVP in the 1968–69 season. Wilt Chamberlain is the only other player to do the same thing. According to the official NBA website, "A 6-foot-7 bull of a center, [Unseld] forged his reputation on relentless rebounding, bone-jarring picks, and laser-beam outlet passes. He did all the unspectacular things that led to glamorous victories." The Bullets had never had a winning season before Unseld's arrival. He helped the team to 10 winning seasons and 12 consecutive playoff appearances. Fittingly, he was named the 1978 championship series MVP as he led the Bullets to their only NBA title.

Known as "The Big E," **ELVIN HAYES** thrilled fans with his dominating style of play.

The Bullets soared to a 57–25 record in Unseld's first season. But the New York Knicks swept them in the first round of the playoffs.

Baltimore lost to the Knicks again in the 1970 playoffs. It got past the Knicks the following season in the Eastern Conference finals. Now the Bullets faced the Milwaukee Bucks for the NBA title. The Bucks swept them. The Knicks again knocked the Bullets out of the playoffs the following two seasons. By then they had added Elvin Hayes. Hayes was a rugged power forward. He and Unseld gave the Bullets a dominating front court. But the team had a serious problem. It still wasn't drawing fans.

The Bullets moved to Landover, Maryland, before the 1973–74 season. Landover is only a few miles from the nation's capital. The team became the Capital Bullets. It won 47 games. Once again, it

A durable forward, **HAYES** never missed more than 2 games in any of his 16 seasons in the NBA.

lost to the Knicks in the playoffs. The Bullets had yet another name change before the next season. Now they were the Washington Bullets. "Located as close as we are to Washington, [D.C.] we think the name Washington is more definitive and provides a clearer identity to our actual location," said owner Abe Pollin. Like Baltimore, Washington had a previous pro hoops history. The Washington Capitols joined the BAA in 1946. In 1949, they joined the NBA. The team folded halfway through the next season.

LEGENDS OF THE HARDWOOD

SINGING A SWEET TUNE

"The opera ain't over 'til the fat lady sings" is one of the most famous sayings in sports. It means there is still a chance of victory, even if a team is behind. The saying became famous during the 1978 playoffs. Coach Dick Motta kept repeating it in the championship series against Seattle. Motta's faith paid off as the Bullets won the title. The phrase had originated with sportswriter Dan Cook two years earlier. Cook repeated it during the 1978 playoffs. Motta heard the phrase and began using it. "It turned into a fun thing to watch—they had contests throughout the championship series of people dressing up as fat ladies," Motta said.

Former Celtics star **K. C. JONES** was known for his laid-back coaching style.

The Bullets surged to a 60–22 record in 1974–75. After two hard-fought playoff series, they advanced to the NBA Finals. Washington was a heavy favorite against the Golden State Warriors. Yet the Warriors swept all four games. Two were decided by a single point. The Warriors won the other two by six and eight points apiece. “It was very hard to take, considering how hard we had worked to get to the Finals,” Hayes said. “I’m not taking anything away from the Warriors, because they were a very good team and very competitive. But there was nobody in our locker room who wouldn’t have wanted another shot at them. Let’s face it: we thought we were better than they were.”

Quick forward **BOB DANDRIDGE** was a key member of the Bullets in their back-to-back Finals appearance.

TAKING THE TITLE

The Bullets had early playoff exits in the next two seasons. Fans had low expectations going into the 1977–78 playoffs. The team had just 44 regular-season wins. "The thing that happened with us that year

Legendary coach **DICK MOTTA** led the Bullets to the playoffs in all four of his years in Washington.

is that we had a lot of injuries and one time we took a trip on the West Coast and I had to use [assistant coach] Bernie Bickerstaff in practice," said coach Dick Motta. "I don't think we were overconfident, but we knew that we had a good team that would take a really good team to knock us out of the championship." Motta increased the intensity as the playoffs began. The Bullets beat the Atlanta Hawks, San Antonio Spurs, and Philadelphia 76ers in the Eastern Conference playoffs. They faced the Seattle SuperSonics for the NBA title. The Sonics took a 3–2 lead.

LEGENDS OF THE HARDWOOD

THE ODD COUPLE

MANUTE BOL, CENTER, 7-FOOT-7, 1985–88

TYRONE "MUGGSY" BOGUES, POINT GUARD, 5-FOOT-3, 1987–88

In the 1987–88 season, Washington had one of the most unusual teammate pairings in NBA history. One was point guard Tyrone "Muggsy" Bogues. Standing just 5-foot-3, he was the shortest-ever NBA player. The other was 7-foot-7 Manute Bol. He was one of the two tallest players in NBA history. Bol was a shot-blocking sensation. He wasn't much of a scorer. In fact, he is the only NBA player to record more blocked shots (2,086) than points scored (1,599). Despite his stature, Bogues had 39 blocked shots in his career. He was much better-known for running the Bullets' offense. The two players had just one season together. They were both traded when it ended.

Bruising swingman **RICK MAHORN** was an intimidating presence on the court.

"IT WAS ALL WORTH IT. FROM THE PAIN OF LOSING TO GOLDEN STATE TO WINNING THE TITLE. THAT'S WHY YOU PLAY THE GAME, AND IT WAS EVEN BETTER THAN YOU THOUGHT IT WOULD BE."

But the Bullets won Game 6 by 35 points. The Bullets took the title by edging the Sonics in Seattle, 105–99. "This is why we hung together and worked so hard," said a joyous Hayes. "It was all worth it. From the pain of losing to Golden State to winning the title. That's why you play the game, and it was even better than you thought it would be."

The Bullets had high expectations of a repeat the following season. They notched the league's best record of 54–28. After series wins over the Hawks and the Spurs, they again faced the Sonics in the Finals. They won the first game, 99–97. But Seattle swept the next four. No one knew it at the time, but Washington's glory days were over. In the next nine seasons, it had winning records just three times. The most notable players during this span were "Bruise Brothers" Jeff Ruland and Rick Mahorn. They played so hard that an announcer called them

"McFilthy and McNasty." "Jeff and I didn't care," Mahorn said. "We played hard because we were going to do anything we could to win. We were not dirty, and we did not try to injure anyone."

The Bullets still made the playoffs in seven of those nine years. They even defeated the New Jersey Nets in the first round of the 1982 playoffs. One of their best performances came in the first round of the 1988 playoffs. The Bullets pushed the heavily favored Detroit Pistons to five games. A one-point loss in Game 2 ultimately cost them the series. That loss launched a long dry spell. The Bullets missed the playoffs eight years in a row after that. During this period, three members of the team were voted as the league's Most Improved Player. When Washington finally returned to the playoffs in 1997, the Chicago Bulls swept the Bullets, 3–0.

Two-time All-Star **JEFF RULAND** didn't let anyone get in his way.

The late 1990s brought a name change to the team but not many winning records.

WELCOMING THE WIZARDS

By the early 1990s, owner Abe Pollin had become alarmed with the association of his team's name and gun violence. Washington, D.C., had the highest homicide rate in the country. His concerns came to a head in 1995. Israel's prime minister, Yitzhak Rabin, was assassinated by a gunman. Rabin had been a

"THE NAME DEPICTS ENERGY AND AN OMNIPRESENT POWER, AND BRINGS TO LIGHT WHAT IS HOPED TO BE THE WISE AND MAGICAL NATURE OF THE TEAM."

close friend of Pollin's. Pollin announced a "rename the team" contest. Entries included Monuments, Antelopes, Funkadelics, Sea Dogs, and Stallions. "Wizards" emerged victorious. It "portrayed a nonviolent image," according to the team's official website. "The name depicts energy and an omnipresent power, and brings to light what is hoped to be the wise and magical nature of the team." Not everyone was pleased. The National Association for the Advancement of Colored People (NAACP) pointed out a less-friendly connection. The head of the racist Ku Klux Klan (KKK) organization is known as the Imperial Wizard. But the name change went ahead. It became official before the 1997–98 season. The team didn't seem wise or magical then. The Wizards went 42–40 and missed the playoffs. They did even worse the following two seasons, finishing low in league standings.

In 2000, the Wizards made headlines by hiring Michael Jordan as team president. He had retired two years earlier from the Bulls. The team also made another kind of headline. Its 19–63 mark in 2000–01 was the worst since its first season as the Chicago Packers. Jordan came out of retirement in 2001. He helped the Wizards nearly double their win total to 37. They also won 37 games the following season. Jordan averaged at least 20 points a game in each season. But Washington still wasn't a playoff contender. Jordan felt his teammates weren't trying hard enough. "I don't see anyone covering my back, as everyone probably expected

Superstar **MICHAEL JORDAN** returned to the court for two years as a Wizards player.

SPELLING IT RIGHT

ANTAWN JAMISON, POWER/SMALL FORWARD, 6-FOOT-8, 2004–10

Antawn Jamison's parents wanted to spell his name Antwan. But the hospital made a mistake. They misspelled his name on his birth certificate. His parents still pronounced it *An-twan*. There was no confusion about his basketball ability. Jamison was the 1998 College Player of the Year. He was Sixth Man of the Year in 2004 when he played for the Dallas Mavericks. He was a two-time All-Star with the Wizards. He also played for the U.S. national team in 2006. Antawn and his wife Ione wanted a "Junior." So they named their first son Antwan—and made sure it was spelled right.

me to cover theirs," he said. "The way we'll be able to turn this around is to go out every night and have the effort. Sometimes, things may not go your way, but the effort should be there every single night." He retired again in 2003. Without Jordan, the team sagged to only 25 wins.

The 2004–05 season marked the start of a new era in Washington. The Wizards had traded for swingman Larry Hughes in 2002 and guard Gilbert Arenas in 2003. Now they acquired forward Antawn Jamison. The three guided the Wizards to a 20-game improvement over the previous season. Washington roped the Bulls in the first round of the playoffs, 4–2. It was its first playoff win since 1982. But the Miami Heat melted the Wizards in the next round. They swept all four games. The Wizards made the playoffs in each of the next three seasons. But they had a new nemesis: the Cleveland Cavaliers. The Cavs eliminated the Wizards in the first round each time.

A double-double threat, center **MARCIN GORTAT** averaged 13.5 points and 10 rebounds per game in 2015–16.

THE GREAT WALL OF WASHINGTON

Arenas missed most of the 2008–09 season with a knee injury. The Wizards limped to a 19–63 record. It was the second-worst regular-season mark in franchise history. Washington wasn't

"WASHINGTON IS REALLY BECOMING GOOD RIGHT BEFORE OUR EYES," SAID CELTICS PRESIDENT DANNY AINGE.

much better the following season. The best thing about that season was winning the top pick in the 2010 Draft. Washington selected University of Kentucky All-American guard John Wall. There weren't enough good players surrounding him. The losing continued. Wall was injured at the start of the 2012–13 season. The Wizards lost their first 12 games without him. They were 5–28 when he returned. They finished the season with a dismal 29–53 record.

The Wizards finally broke the cycle of losing with a 44–38 mark in 2013–14. One reason for the improvement was center Marcin Gortat. He came to the Wizards in a trade with Phoenix. He averaged 13 points and 10 rebounds a game. Another was second-year shooting guard Bradley Beal. And Wall lived up to his high expectations. He became an All-Star for the first time. The Wizards easily defeated Chicago in the playoffs. But the Indiana Pacers knocked them off in the next round.

Many people regarded it as a team on the rise. "Washington is really becoming good right before our eyes," said Celtics president Danny Ainge before the 2014–15 season. "They improved a lot last year, and I think they're going to be a team that's going to be very good in the East. I think Chicago is terrific, and of course Cleveland—I think those are probably the top three teams in the East." The Wizards didn't quite live up to those lofty expectations. They finished with a 46–36 record. That put them fifth in the Eastern Conference. They swept the Toronto

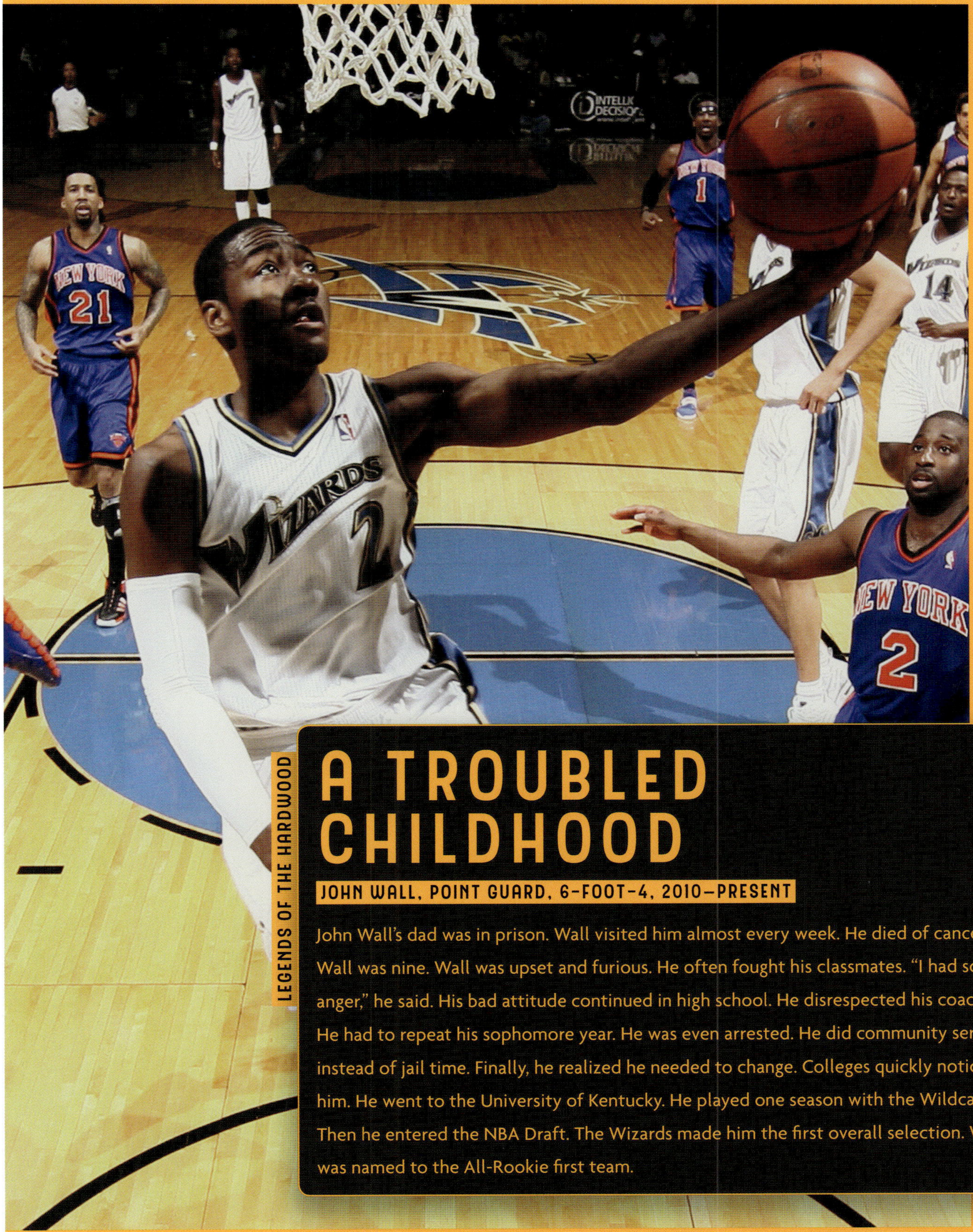

A TROUBLED CHILDHOOD

JOHN WALL, POINT GUARD, 6-FOOT-4, 2010–PRESENT

John Wall's dad was in prison. Wall visited him almost every week. He died of cancer when Wall was nine. Wall was upset and furious. He often fought his classmates. "I had so much anger," he said. His bad attitude continued in high school. He disrespected his coaches. He had to repeat his sophomore year. He was even arrested. He did community service instead of jail time. Finally, he realized he needed to change. Colleges quickly noticed him. He went to the University of Kentucky. He played one season with the Wildcats. Then he entered the NBA Draft. The Wizards made him the first overall selection. Wall was named to the All-Rookie first team.

After a five-year drought, the Wizards returned to the playoffs in 2014 but stalled in the second round.

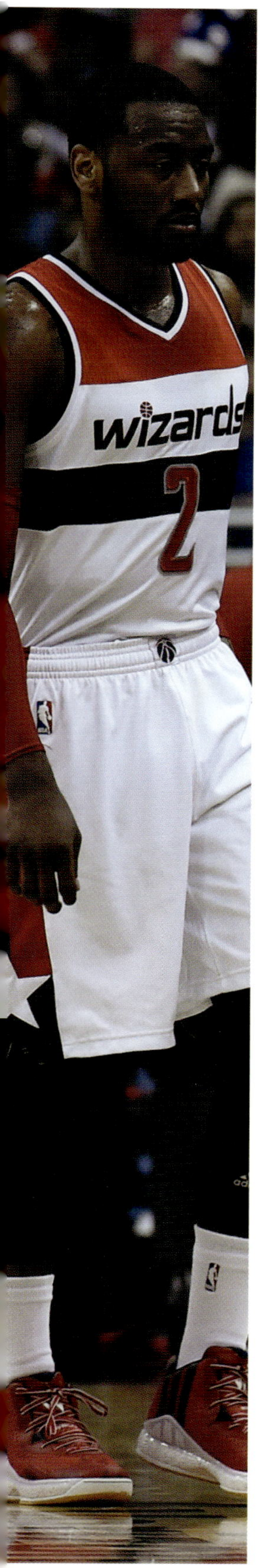

Raptors in the first round. In the second round, they took a 2–1 lead over the top-seeded Hawks. But they suffered three heartbreaking defeats in a row. They lost those games by five points, one point, and three points. Fans expected this recent run of success to continue in 2015–16. But after a 6–4 start, the Wizards spent nearly all of the remainder of the season slightly under the .500 level. Five times they rose to .500. But they could never get past that hump. Their 41–41 record missed the playoffs by three games. Washington improved to 49–33 in 2016–17 to win its division. Wall staked a claim to being the Eastern Conference's best point guard by averaging a career-high 23.1 points a game and 10.7 assists. "He was the Wizards' catalyst all season long," remarked Matt Ellentuck of MSN Sports. The Wizards brushed aside Atlanta in the first round of the playoffs and pushed Boston to a deciding Game 7 in the conference semifinals before falling just short of victory.

Washington fans endured one of the most dismal stretches in NBA history. Since 2013, hopes along the Potomac River have started to rise. Many people think the Wizards have most of the pieces in place to become a genuine contender. Adding an outstanding rookie or prized free agent would give them an excellent chance of a deep playoff run. Fans would love to see another championship banner fly high.

SELECTED BIBLIOGRAPHY

Ballard, Chris. *The Art of a Beautiful Game: The Thinking Fan's Tour of the NBA*. New York: Simon & Schuster, 2010.

Hareas, John. *Ultimate Basketball: More Than 100 Years of the Sport's Evolution*. New York: DK, 2004.

Hubbard, Jan, ed. *The Official NBA Basketball Encyclopedia*. 3rd edition. New York: Doubleday, 2000.

NBA.com. "Washington Wizards." http://www.nba.com/wizards/.

Simmons, Bill. *The Book of Basketball: The NBA According to the Sports Guy*. New York: Ballantine, 2009.

WEBSITES

THE MEANING OF MIYAH

http://ftw.usatoday.com/2016/02/john-wall-miyah-cancer-espn-sportscenter-video

This video shows the deeply caring relationship between the Wizards' John Wall and Miyah Telemaque-Nelson.

WASHINGTON WIZARDS KIDS FAN CLUB

http://www.nba.com/wizards/kids-club-membership

Free membership in the Wizards Fan Club includes a monthly newsletter and contests.

Note: Every effort has been made to ensure that any websites listed above were active at the time of publication. However, because of the nature of the Internet, it is impossible to guarantee that these sites will remain active indefinitely or that their contents will not be altered.

INDEX